The
Fresh Flower
Project Book

Joanna Sheen

MEREHURST

Published in 1993 by Merehurst Limited
Ferry House, 51-57 Lacy Road, Putney, London SW15 1PR
Text © copyright Joanna Sheen 1993
Photographs © copyright Merehurst Limited 1993

ISBN 1-85391-237-9

A catalogue record for this book is available from the British Library.

Managing Editor **Heather Dewhurst**
Edited by **Diana Lodge**
Designed by **Lisa Tai**
Photography by **Debbie Patterson**
Styling assistant **Camilla Bambrough**

Acknowledgements
Merehurst would like to thank the following for loaning props for photography: The Dining Room
Shop, 62-64 White Hart Lane, London SW13; Georgina Von Etzdorf, 149 Sloane Street, London
SW1; Modus Vicendi, Stand GO, 80 Ground Floor, Alfies Antique Market, Church Street, London
NW1; Paperchase, 213 Tottenham Court Road, London W1; Tobias & the Angel, 68 White Hart
Lane, London SW13.

Typesetting by **Litho Link Limited**
Colour separation by **Fotographics Ltd UK – Hong Kong**
Printed in Italy by **New Interlitho S.p.A.**

*Merehurst is a leading publisher of craft books and has an excellent range of titles
to suit all levels. Please send to the address above for our free catalogue, stating
the title of this book.*

Contents

Introduction

Flowers are one of Nature's greatest creations and the enjoyment and beauty they can bring is immense. There is absolutely no need to have any talent for flower arranging, just the gift of enjoying beautiful things. Flowers can be as inspiring placed in a clean jam jar as worked on for hours in a complicated arrangement. The most important thing is to treat the flowers correctly, which includes keeping their water topped up so that they can last as long as possible.

If you want to go further than admiring flowers in a jam jar, then arranging flowers with complementary foliage, and other colours and textures can be a very exciting pastime. There is no limit to the time you can spend arranging flowers; you can achieve simple ideas in minutes, or pass an enjoyable morning creating a masterpiece – the choice is yours! This book includes a range of projects, from simple floating flowers, to more advanced ideas for filling a fireplace or decorating a Christmas topiary tree.

Conditioning flowers and foliage

The first and most important point, whether you are gathering the flowers and foliage from your garden or purchasing them from a florist, is to treat them correctly to prolong their life as much as possible. If you are buying flowers from a good florist, they should be well conditioned already, but it is better to be safe than sorry.

Flowers should all be cleanly cut with a sharp pair of scissors, rather than sawn or tugged at with fingers or a blunt knife. Do not crush the stems of flowers as this merely damages them and prevents them from drinking water – a clean cut will work much more effectively. Although this is not always possible, it is preferable to cut the stem under water, the reason being that this will stop any air bubbles from travelling up the stem and preventing a good flow of water. In practice, however, I usually cut the stems quickly and get them under water as soon as possible. Cut the stems at an angle to help them drink the water; if a stem is cut flat and the cut end touches the bottom of the vase, this will limit the amount of water that can be taken up.

Once the stems have been cut at an angle and any surplus foliage removed, they should be placed in deep water so that they can have a long drink before being placed in a vase. If, however, you are going to put them in a simple arrangement that will allow them free access to plenty of water, then you could skip this step. Foliage and flowers cut from the garden should definitely be placed in deep water and preferably left for several hours; I would leave foliage overnight.

FLOWER FOOD

There is no need to use an expensive flower food – if the florist gives you some with the flowers, then by all means use it, but otherwise you can make your own mixture. Fill half the vase with lemonade and half with fresh tap water, then add one drop of household bleach. This will prevent any build up of bacteria in the vase, and the sugar in the lemonade will feed the flowers. There are many suggestions for flower food, but this mixture seems to work well with many varieties and helps to prolong their life. If you have particularly long-lasting flowers, which seem happy to go into a second week on display, change the water after five days and cut the stems again; this will enable the flowers to continue drinking the water and food efficiently.

EQUIPMENT

There are a few pieces of equipment that are useful when arranging fresh flowers, although a small collection of vases is basically sufficient. Florist's foam is widely available and makes flower arranging so much easier. If you use foam in an arrangement, or an arrangement is delivered to you from a florist in foam, then keep topping up the water regularly as it will dry out quite rapidly. Wires in varying thicknesses are useful, especially a small reel of silver-coloured rose wire.

Individual accessories will depend upon the project you want to undertake, and in this book they are all listed where necessary. It is worth collecting a small store of useful accessories as and

Collect useful odds and ends for flower arranging gradually, as and when you see them.

when you see them, for instance while visiting a garden centre or craft store. If you have a box of 'useful' things, you will be spared from making a special journey when you want to try a new type of arrangement. Candle holders, for example, are well worth buying. They are not expensive; they can be used many times, and they will hold candles safely and securely in either fresh or dried arrangements. (Leaning candles can spoil a display, as they catch the eye more than the flowers.)

Baskets and jugs are another item that can be collected whenever you find a good source. Unfortunately, a good basket collection may pose storage problems, but small containers in general are always useful and take up less space.

Flowers from a florist are obviously quite an expense if bought on a regular basis. Growing them in the garden is a wonderful alternative. However, I often find that keen gardeners will not pick flowers for the house and prefer to leave them in the garden, which leads you back to square one. My suggestion would be to have a few flowers that are for cutting, but to concentrate on growing various types of foliage in the garden for use in arrangements. It is very difficult to obtain any selection of greenery at all from most florists, apart from ferns, eucalyptus and one or two other options.

If you have a good selection of foliage in your garden, you will be able to spend a reasonable sum buying a few choice flowers and fill your arrangements with many lovely and unusual pieces of greenery. An arrangement containing only a selection of foliage can look truly beautiful, and you may prefer this type of design at times!

Daisy garland

Garlands of flowers decorating an entrance or gate can make a stunning focal point. Although they look complicated and expensive, they are neither; with some patience and a reasonable collection of material, they can be made in a few hours and will gather an enormous number of compliments!

$\mathscr{D}$aisy garland

Many different ingredients are suitable for inclusion in a garland. You will need several types of foliage, as these act as useful padding, and some fairly solid flowers – dainty ones can be missed among the collection of ingredients. Roses always look lovely, but they are an expensive choice, as you would need about two dozen at least for a garland of this size. Using daisy sprays, however, as I have here, you can produce a lovely effect for a modest cost. You will need a large bunch of both pink and white daisies (enough to produce about 36 heads of each), a bunch of eucalyptus, senecio and some conifer, rosemary and a small bunch of gypsophila. This would be enough to produce a garland approximately 1m (3ft) in length.

INGREDIENTS

Flowers and foliage,
as above

❧

1.3m (4ft) of dressing
gown cord

❧

2m (6ft) of ribbon,
4–5cm (1½–2in) wide

❧

One reel of rose wire

1 Form each of the ingredients into about 12 small bunches, some 5–7.5cm (2–3in) long. The daisies should have three heads per bunch, and the other bunches should be roughly the same size. Make a loop at each end of the cord and bind with wire; bind on the first few bunches of foliage, making sure you have a well-balanced effect.

2 It is easier to use pieces of reel wire approximately 30cm (12in) long rather than one long continuous piece, which might get knotted and tangled around the garland. Continue to bind on the bunches randomly, but always taking care that they are evenly distributed. Keep the bunches on top of the cord; do not allow it to slide so that you are binding bunches all around the cord, as you would require much more material to make a garland with flowers or foliage all around. If the garland will be viewed from the front and back, double the quantities.

3 Once you have covered a quarter of the cord, start again from the opposite end and work towards the middle. Continue adding bunches and binding firmly, keeping the stems on top of the cord. As you approach the middle (you can mark this with a small twist of wire), shorten the length of the stems and place them almost at right angles to the cord. Lay the finished garland out and check that there are no bald patches and the width is even. Make two loops and tails from the ribbon (see page 48) and wire them into each end at the base of the cord loops.

A fireplace arrangement

The fireplace is often the focal point in a room, and can look very dull when unlit. During the summer months a dried flower arrangement looks lovely, but for special occasions a display of fresh flowers is a real talking point.

73-76

$\mathscr{A}$ fireplace arrangement

If you have access to flowers from your garden, even a large arrangement such as this can cost very little to put together. The copper container can double as a coal scuttle or log container when it is not in use as a vase! Foliage is very important to help fill an arrangement like this one; a design made with flowers on their own would use many more blooms than I have included here. If you enjoy having fresh flowers in the house, a good selection of foliage plants and shrubs in the garden is invaluable. This arrangement uses three bunches of eucalyptus, four bunches of red freesias, five stems of apricot-coloured single chrysanthemums, and five stems of orange lilies.

INGREDIENTS

Flowers and foliage,
see above

ର

A large copper container,
30cm (12in) in diameter

ର

Five blocks of green
florist's foam

1 Place the foam in the container – lining it first if there are any holes in the metal, and cutting the blocks if necessary. Add water, allowing it to soak into the foam. Insert the eucalyptus, making a fan with the highest point in the middle and the longest points at each side.

2 Cut a stem of chrysanthemum to the correct length – it should come just below the height of the longest piece of eucalyptus at the back. Clean away all the leaves that would go into the foam. Do likewise with the other pieces of chrysanthemum at the sides and front.

3 The orange lilies go into the arrangement next; again, trim off any excess leaves at the base of each stem and cut it to the correct length by holding it roughly in position and allowing about 2.5–5cm (1–2in) to go into the foam. Place all the lily stems into the arrangement.

4 Finally, insert the freesias. You will not need to trim the stems very much. They should be put in the main body of the arrangement to add a darker colour. If you are unable to get these particular flowers, you could use either yellow freesias or golden chrysanthemums as a substitute.

Marble display

These flattened nuggets have gained tremendous popularity over the last few years. They are invaluable if you want to use a clear container to arrange flowers, as they cover the stems and hold them in place as well as looking attractive.

$\mathcal{M}$arble display

Simple arrangements are often the prettiest and time is precious to us all. An arrangement like this can be made in a very short time and appreciated for at least a week. Using marbles or nuggets as a flower arranging aid is a relatively new idea and is now becoming very popular. They overcome the problem of unsightly stalks being visible when you use a clear glass container and they hold the stems in position, making arranging much easier (for suppliers, see page 48). Any flowers could be used in an arrangement like this, but the lilies and Singapore orchids used here last well. I have used three bunches (three stems in a bunch) of Singapore orchids and three stems of white lilies.

INGREDIENTS

Flowers and foliage,
see above

❧

Glass vase or jug

❧

Two jars of glass nuggets
(the exact quantity depends
upon the size of the vase)

1 Fill the container about two-thirds full with nuggets and add water until the level is just above the nuggets. The foliage used here are the ferns and leaves that come with the bunch of Singapore orchids. I used six pieces, pushing them into the nuggets and splaying them in a fan.

2 *Put the three stems of white lilies in position, forming a rough triangle. Make sure that you have taken off any leaves that would go below the surface of the water, as these would make the water smell after a short while.*

3 *Add the white Singapore orchids, one stem at a time. Make sure that the stems are held by the nuggets and place them all around the lilies. These orchids are not as expensive as they sound; the small bunches of three stems are readily available now, and are reasonably priced.*

Anemones in terracotta

Terracotta is usually regarded as suitable for outdoor use, but it can look stunning when used for informal arrangements indoors. Either waterproof the container by coating the inside with PVA adhesive and blocking the hole in the base or, much more simply, put your flowers in a jam jar hidden inside the container. Garden flowers are ideal for this type of arrangement, but something simple from a florist could also be attractive.

INGREDIENTS

12–15 Helleborus foetidus
leaves

✌

3–4 bunches of mixed
anemones

✌

One jam jar (or seal the
container, see above)

✌

One terracotta pot

1 Clean the pot if it has been outside, but do not scrub too hard as the discoloration is most attractive. Place the jam jar inside the pot (or waterproof as mentioned above) and fill with water. Place the leaves around the pot in a random way to form a base for the flowers.

2 Place flowers in the container one at a time, mixing the colours randomly. Ensure that the stems are well down into the jar so that they can take up plenty of water. This is an informal arrangement, and the look should be natural – the backs of flowers and curves of stems can be as attractive as the full face.

Rustic basket

This rough country basket looks wonderful when casually filled with a collection of spring flowers. Rustic baskets and containers add so much to an informal arrangement of this type, and baskets are usually fairly easily available. Once you have built up a collection, they can be used over and over again!

Rustic basket

Spring flowers are always beautiful, whether they are artistically arranged or just a bunch of daffodils abandoned in a jam jar. The strong colours of the yellow miniature daffodils in this arrangement would brighten any corner of the house. The foliage is taken from the garden – trailing ivy, *Helleborus foetidus* foliage and flowers, and some pussy willow. This choice, however, is easily interchangeable with whatever foliage is readily available to you, whether it be garden bits and pieces or ferns and eucalyptus from a florist. The blue grape hyacinths make a lovely contrast against the yellow and green, but again another small spring flower could be used instead.

INGREDIENTS

10–12 Helleborus foetidus leaves and flowers, small bunch of pussy willow, 7 pieces of trailing ivy and 5 of spurge (euphorbia), 9 miniature daffodils, 9 blue grape hyacinths, and a few strands of bear grass

Half block of green florist's foam

Rustic basket, 20cm (8in) in diameter

1 Soak the foam until it has taken up as much water as possible. Line the basket very carefully with polythene (this one came with a plastic lining), and then wedge the foam in the basket. Cover the foam with the hellebore leaves, set at various angles.

2 Add the other foliage ingredients. First, put the pussy willow at the back of the arrangement and at the front; then some trailing pieces of ivy; some spurge goes in the centre at the back, and some nearer the front. The hellebore flowers are then added to the centre of the arrangement.

3 Finally, add the remaining flowers in groups, varying the lengths of the stems so that they do not look too regimented. You could use more or less of any of these ingredients, depending upon availability. As a finishing touch, add some wispy strands of bear grass or other fine grass to lend a delicate feel to the edges of the arrangement.

Table centre

Beeswax candles burn with a sweet smell and, together with the rosemary, add a lovely gentle fragrance to set the mood at a dinner party. Take care to keep the height of the arrangement fairly low or you will block everyone's view.

$\mathcal{T}$able centre

The centre of the table can also be the centre of attraction at a dinner party if you can find a few moments earlier in the day to prepare a small flower arrangement. Candles are always successful, and remember to include plenty of foliage as it makes a lovely background to the flowers. Given the choice I would leave out the flowers rather than the foliage! You will need a bunch of rosemary, a bunch of pink alstroemeria, 12–15 medium-to-large ivy leaves, about six trailing pieces of ivy (preferably with berries), and nine pink roses.

INGREDIENTS

Flowers and foliage,
see above

Three candleholders
and candles

A half block of green
florist's foam

One shallow basket

1 *Line the basket with plastic and soak the foam. Place the foam in the basket and push the pointed green candle holders* *into the foam. Cover the foam completely with ivy leaves, and have trails of ivy coming out of each end of the arrangement.*

2 *Add more ivy berries, if you have them, and some of the rosemary. The alstroemeria can be cut fairly short and placed in the arrangement one flower at a time rather than as a spray. If you cannot obtain rosemary, then use any other sweetly-scented herbal foliage, such as mint, sage, thyme or lavender. Make sure all foliage is well conditioned before you use it so that it doesn't droop before the party.*

3 *Lighten the arrangement with some sprigs of rosemary and then add the roses, placing them fairly low, where they will be seen. Check that the*

arrangement looks pretty from all angles, as your guests are going to be sitting down and looking across at it from all sides. If you make the

arrangement standing up, you may find, when you join your guests at dinner and look across the table, that you have left a large gap in the flowers!

Tied bunch

There are several occasions for which you might want to make an informal bouquet – as a presentation after a speech, for example, for a wedding or other celebration, or simply as a thank-you present. Once you have mastered the technique of binding the flowers firmly, this style of bouquet is simple to produce yourself.

Tied bunch

Many people prefer to use a minimal amount of foliage in bouquets and arrangements, but I think the foliage is just as important as the flowers and provides the green, grey or autumnal colours that act as a foil for the tones of the flowers. This bunch uses flowering privet and *Lonicera purpusii*, the latter having leaves of a clear lime green which works well with the intense pink of the roses and the strong blue of the iris. The flowering currant (*Ribes sanguineum*) adds a charmingly informal garden touch to the bouquet and takes some of the emphasis away from the more commercial flowers. You will need one bunch (10–12 stems) of iris, seven pink roses, seven to nine stems of mixed foliage and five stems of flowering currant.

INGREDIENTS

*Flowers and foliage
(see above)*

❧

One reel of rose wire

❧

*1m (3ft) each of two
toning colours of ribbon,
2.5cm (1in) wide*

1 Lay out the foliage, with the longest piece in the centre and a slightly shorter piece each side. Bind the first few pieces firmly with wire, and add more pieces at an angle, keeping a fan shape so the ingredients do not overlap.

2 Place some irises between the pieces of foliage, cutting them to different lengths. You could use other flowers instead of this combination, but try to maintain a contrast of shapes, with at least one longer or pointed type of flower and something round if you are replacing the roses.

3 The roses can be placed in position next. Bind the wire firmly around one point after each stem or every two or three stems, depending on how confident you feel. Do not lose any of the flowers by burying them in the foliage; in particular, make sure all the roses are visible, as they are the star flowers in the bouquet. Although this example uses only three different types of flower, you could easily produce a beautiful tied bunch using bits and pieces from the garden.

4 Finally, add the flowering currant, which softens the bunch and should be distributed evenly throughout the design. Bind it in firmly and then cut the wire and tuck it into the bunch. Cover the wire by tying the two ribbons simultaneously around the bunch at the point where you have been binding. Make a large bow, and then cut the ends of the ribbon at an angle.

Floating flowers

The simplest of arrangements can often be the most effective. Nothing could be easier than to float a few beautiful flower heads in some shallow water, and the end result is quite lovely. Select a container deep enough to allow the flowers to float, as opposed to resting on the bottom, and make sure the interior of the container is perfect, as it will be visible in parts. The choice of blooms will depend upon the flowers you have available in the garden or the selection at the florist. Pick an open-faced flat flower so that it looks good from overhead as opposed to a sideways view. The number of flower heads will depend upon the size of your container.

INGREDIENTS

Flower heads and leaves of your choice – in this case five camellias and their leaves

A shallow waterproof container

Clean the container thoroughly; dry it, then fill with water to a depth of about two thirds. Cut the stems fairly short, but not so close to the back of the flower that you risk it falling to pieces. Any leaves can be cut off the stalks individually and floated around the flowers. To add an extra dimension you could include some floating candles in the arrangement or choose flowers of different colours.

A circular arrangement

This would make a delightful table centre or could be placed on a coffee table or hearth. The ingredients are simple and inexpensive, but the end result is charming. The arrangement is made with wet florist's foam, so it is also long lasting.

$\mathscr{A}$ circular arrangement

This natural design, reminiscent of woodland glades or streams, would be ideal as a table centre as it is so low. The ring of foam is available from florists' or other craft stores and comes in a plastic dish, so it needs no other base. You could use any type of moss; the varieties used here are bun moss and reindeer moss, but all types would be suitable. Moss can be dried and then resuscitated, becoming bright green again very easily. The stones could be replaced by small shells or cones, and obviously any other flowers could be substituted for the white daisies. I have used two stems of white single chrysanthemums, a large sprig of eucalyptus, some prostrate juniper, and the two varieties of moss.

INGREDIENTS

Flowers and foliage,
see above

❧

Moss (two types used here)

❧

Stones

❧

0.71mm (22 gauge) stub
wires, in 7.5cm (3in)
lengths

❧

Green foam ring,
25cm (10in) in diameter

1 Soak the foam well, holding it under the tap. Bend the wires into hairpin shapes. Using flexible pieces of moss to cover the inner foam, hairpin the moss to the foam. Cover the ring with the mosses, leaving spaces for flowers.

2 *Continue around the ring, inserting the juniper by pushing small stems into the foam. Add the eucalyptus, either at an angle or straight in like the juniper.*

3 *Cut the chrysanthemum stems very short – about 5cm (2in) long – and place them around the ring. Remember to decorate the outer edge of the foam, as this will be seen as much as the top. A smaller version could be made using small clumps of lawn daisies.*

$\mathscr{A}$ basket for a bedroom

A basket of flowers looks wonderful anywhere in the house, but seems particularly welcoming in a bedroom. If this colour scheme does not match your decor, you could substitute cream orchids and change the colours of the other flowers. As it is made with wet foam, this arrangement should last well, providing you have conditioned the foliage and flowers carefully before using them. You will need from 20 to 30 pieces of assorted foliage, about 15cm (6in) long; I have used silvery *Atriplex halimus*, *Vibernum tinus* 'Variegata' and eucalyptus. The flowers in the basket are a bunch of yellow and red Singapore orchids, a small bunch of yellow alstroemeria and ten apricot roses.

INGREDIENTS

Flowers and foliage,
see above

ﻬ

A half block of green
florist's foam

ﻬ

A basket, about 20cm (8in)
in diameter

1 If unlined, line the basket with polythene. Soak the foam and place it in the basket. Insert the foliage evenly, hiding most of the foam and putting some shorter pieces at the top. Add the orchids, breaking sprays into individual flowers.

2 Add the alstroemeria, again using separate flowers rather than whole sprays. Finish with the apricot roses, trimming the stems to about 10–12.5cm (4–5in) and removing any leaves and thorns.

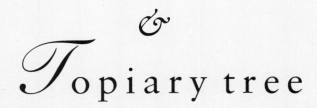

Christmas wreath
&
Topiary tree

Christmas is a time when all those who love flowers like to decorate the home and make welcoming arrangements for guests and family. Red and green are the traditional Christmas colours and have been used here to create a very special wreath for the door and a fabulous topiary tree.

Christmas wreath

This wreath has florist's foam wired to the base to give the flowers some water, prolonging the life of the arrangement. Evergreen foliage lasts well on a wreath, even without a supply of water, but the roses will last much longer if the foam is kept wet. Once the roses are past their best, they can be removed and more foliage added to keep the wreath going. A red ribbon could be used to add colour instead. Here, I have used three or four sprays of holly, five trailing pieces of ivy, a few sprigs of prostrate juniper, a handful of telancia moss and nine red roses.

INGREDIENTS

Flowers and foliage,
see above

ஃ

Small piece of green
florist's foam

ஃ

A reel of rose wire

ஃ

0.71mm (22 gauge)
stub wires

ஃ

A twig wreath, 30cm (12in)
in diameter

1 Gently, to avoid slicing it, tie the soaked foam to the face of the ring with rose wire. Twist a couple of stub wires around the ring and foam. Insert the base of each ivy stem into the foam and wind the trails around the wreath.

2 *Add the holly and the juniper, pushing the base of each stem gently into the foam. Use some individual leaves to cover the foam, then intertwine some telancia moss into the leaves or around the wreath. If you can't find this particular moss, it could be omitted.*

3 *Finally, add the roses. Remove all the rose leaves and cut the stems to the correct length by holding each flower near the position where you want it; about 12mm (½in) of the stem will be pushed into the foam. Make sure the flowers have been well conditioned (see page 48).*

$\mathcal{T}$opiary tree

Once a tree base has been made, you can use it over and over again, so it is a good investment!
You will need a 15cm (6in) flowerpot and some quick-drying cement. Cover the hole in the
bottom with card; fill the pot between half and two-thirds full with cement, and place a twig or
piece of dowelling, some 45cm (18in) long, into the centre of the cement. Support the twig until
the cement is dry enough to hold it in position. Leave the base to dry for a couple of days before
you use it. You will also need about 30 red roses, 20 small sprigs of holly and of variegated box,
three or four trails of ivy, and some moss (here, bun moss, soaked in water).

INGREDIENTS

Flowers and foliage,
see above

ﾐ

Moss

ﾐ

Tree base, see above

ﾐ

Green florist's foam ball,
15cm (6in) in diameter

ﾐ

Half a block of green
florist's foam, for the base

ﾐ

1m (3ft) of chiffon ribbon,
4cm (1½in) wide, and one
0.56mm (24 gauge) stub
wire

*1 Cover the cement base with
soaked foam. Push the ball
onto the twig, until the twig is
at least half way through.
Twist the ivy stems around the
twig to soften it, and push the
stems into the foam. Cover the
base with moss.*

*2 Cover the ball with sprigs of
holly and place some in the
base. In place of the variegated
box, you could use variegated
holly, if this is available, and a
plainer foliage. Large ivy
leaves would also cover the
ball well.*

3 *Put the sprigs of box between the holly, taking care not to stab yourself with the prickles of the holly. Make sure that the foam is completely covered – bald patches or glimpses of foam between the flowers are not very attractive.*

4 *Finally, put in the roses. Make sure they have been well conditioned so that they last well, and cut the stems to a length of about 5cm (2in). Place the roses evenly all over the ball, and also put some in the base. Although this example uses only one variety of red rose, you could mix these with some deeper red roses or some brighter, more orange roses if you wanted to add more colour variations. Make the ribbon into a bow with streamers (see page 48), and push the ends of the stub wire securing the bow into the foam at the top of the 'trunk'.*

$\mathcal{N}$otes on conditioning

CHRYSANTHEMUMS

Remove as much foliage as possible as this usually dies before the flowers are over. Re-cut the ends of the stems to maintain the flow of water and remove any particularly woody pieces which would prevent water flowing up the stem. Do not crush or split stems – if you cut them this way they will last longer.

HYDRANGEAS

These flowers wilt very easily. You can try to prevent premature wilting either by immersing the ends of the stems in boiling water or by burning the ends with a cigarette lighter before placing the stems in deep water.

LILIES

Take great care with the pollen from lily stamens as it stains clothes and furnishings. If you wish, you can remove the stamens without harming the flower.

ROSES

Remove any lower leaves and snip off the thorns to protect your hands and clothes; when removing thorns, however, do not damage the stem, cut just away from the bark. Never crush the stem ends, as this reduces the life of the flower – re-cut the ends of the stems frequently to ensure that they drink plenty of water. In desperation, try immersing the entire flower in water at room temperature for a few hours to revive a wilted bloom.

SUPPLIERS OF GLASS NUGGETS

House of Marbles, Teign Valley Glass, The Old Pottery, Pottery Road, Bovey Tracey, Devon TQ13 9DS
Factory shop open Mon-Sat 9.00 – 5.00

To make a bow, take a length of ribbon and fold it into loops, as shown. Bind the loops at one end with a stub wire, and use the ends of the wire to insert the bow into the arrangement.